Fifth impression 2020
First paperback edition published in 2018 by
David Philip Publishers, Unit 13, Athlone Industrial Park,
10 Mymoena Crescent, Cape Town, 7764

Hardcover ISBN: 978-1-4856-2489-9
Paperback ISBN: 978-1-4856-2608-4
E pub ISBN: 978-1-4856-2490-5
E mobi ISBN: 978-1-4856-2491-2

Editor: Dusanka Stojakovic and Nicola Rijsdijk
Proofreader: Lauren Ellwood
Typesetting: Electric Book Works

Photographs:
© 2011 JonRichfield Bradypodion pumilum Cape chameleon mature female
© 2005 Mark M. Sykes FBIPP FRPS
© 2005 George Chaplin Predicted skin colour map
© Gallo Images/Foto24/Loanna Hoffman / Thuli Madonsela
© Gisele Wulfsohn / South Photographs / Africa Media Online / Nelson Mandela
© Gallo Images/WireImage/Jim Spellman/ Trevor Noah
© Drum Stories / Bailey's African History Archive / Albertina Sisulu
© Gallo Images/Sunday Times/ Waldo Swiegers / Siyabulela Xusa
© Sue Kramer / Africa Media / Desmond Tutu
© 2005 George Chaplin UVR map
© 2011 Jeanne Waite Follett
© 2012 Marian Vanhaeren & Christopher S. Henshilwood / Beads
© 2011 Magnus Haaland / Bifaces
Portrait of Immanuel Kant by Johann Gottlieb Becker, 1768
Portrait of David Hume by Allan Ramsay, 1766
© 2012 U.S. Air Force photo/Staff Sgt. Benjamin Wilson / blue background was added

Printed and bound in the Republic of South Africa.
David Philip is committed to a sustainable future for our business, our readers and our planet.

Skin we are in

SINDIWE MAGONA
NINA G JABLONSKI

Illustrations by Lynn Fellman

Joshua's
car repair
079-674-0000

iv

ACKNOWLEDGEMENTS

The contributors thank Koos Bekker for his support of this project since its inception, and for the contribution from the Babylonstoren Trust that made its realization possible. They thank their publisher, Dusanka Stojakovic, for her sustained interest, support, and critical feedback on all aspects of content, and three anonymous reviewers for their constructive and insightful suggestions for improvement. Finally, Jablonski thanks the Stellenbosch Institute for Advanced Study and its Director, Hendrik B. Geyer, for continuing support throughout the duration of the project.

SINDIWE MAGONA

is a Writer-in-Residence at the University of the Western Cape, and has won numerous awards in her lifetime, including the Order of Ikhamanga (2011). Magona has written over 120 children's books. Her latest novel, *Chasing the Tails of My Father's Cattle!*, came out in November 2015.

NINA G JABLONSKI

is an anthropologist, paleontologist, and science educator. She studies and writes about human and primate evolution, and is especially interested in how skin and skin colour have evolved and influenced human life and societies. She conducts research and lectures in many countries, including South Africa, where she is a Permanent Fellow of the Stellenbosch Institute for Advanced Study.

LYNN FELLMAN

is a multimedia artist and science communicator. She is an Artist-in-Residence at Cold Spring Harbor Laboratory and a Fulbright Senior Scholar who studies, draws, paints, and lectures about the wonder and beauty of biological science. Her work shows the many layers of connections between people alive today and their ancient ancestors.

He mustn't hear me breathe.

Njabulo stands stock-still, eyes pinned to the slow-slow movement. He knows it's going to happen, but when it does, he is still surprised. Dog-biscuit brown to spring-leaf yellow, he watches the clever chameleon change colour.

But Njabulo is still feeling nervous, waiting under the shade of a tree in his uncle's scrapyard. His friends are on their way over ...

Well, sure, they all go to school together and they're pretty friendly, but they aren't exactly his friends.

Last week Mr Leon set a project on recycling and divided the class into groups. When Njabulo's group heard about his uncle's scrapyard, they decided that would be a great place to work on their project – there were sure to be handy materials there!

But it's not the project Njabulo is worried about ...

Colour is everywhere

The natural world is full of colour, and most plants and animals —
including people — are colourful. The materials that create colour in
nature are called pigments. They serve important functions and are
decorative too. The same pigments have been used over and over for
millions of years in evolution because they work so well.

The chameleon is special because it can change colour depending on
its mood and surroundings. Beneath its transparent outer skin, it has
specialised cells that each contain pigment granules.

When the granules change their position, the chameleon can look light,
dark or brightly coloured. People and most other animals don't have
this amazing ability, and must learn to live with the beautiful skin they
are born with.

"Lovely, isn't he?"

Seeing the chameleon, Uncle Joshua comes over and lays a big hand softly on Njabulo's shoulder. Then he takes a long look at his nephew, and it's as if he knows exactly what he is thinking. "Relax, Njabulo – it's going to be okay. You're going to have a great afternoon."

Njabulo is not so sure. His eyes wander back to the little creature on the leaf. "Uncle Joshua, why can't we all change colour like the chameleon?"

Uncle Joshua looks surprised at first, and then he frowns. "You want to change your skin colour? Now why would you want to do something like that?"

Why can't we change colour?

Our skin gets its colour mostly from the pigments, melanin and haemoglobin. These molecules are called pigments because they have natural colour. Melanin is produced in special cells within the skin, and haemoglobin is carried in the red blood cells found in the small blood vessels deep within our skin. Melanin is the most obvious and important pigment in the skin, and when a person has a lot of it, their skin is darker.

The amount of melanin a person has is controlled by specific genes in their DNA that they inherit from their parents. Most of these genes are dedicated mainly to producing skin colour. They don't determine any other features of a person's body or their behaviour.

Just because someone has a particular skin colour doesn't mean they are going to look or act any particular way. Skin colour just happens to be something we tend to notice.

surface

melanosomes

melanocytes

A blush creeps up Njabulo's neck.
"It's just …" Njabulo mumbles. "Sometimes
I just want to be … to be different."

"Different?" asks Uncle Joshua.

"I want to be clever."

Uncle Joshua's eyebrows rise slightly and it
takes a moment before he replies. "But being
clever doesn't come from the colour of your
skin – surely you know that?"

All people are clever in their own way

All people are clever by nature and have the same big brains. Brain
power isn't related to skin colour, or to the shape of your skull or nose,
or to any other physical feature. The idea that cleverness is associated
with physical features became popular over 200 years ago.

It was put forward mostly by European men who wanted to prove
their own superiority and to rank the people of the rest of the world
below them. These kind of ideas were used to justify their taking
people as slaves.

Modern science provides undeniable evidence that all people are
clever and creative, and that they have the capacity to think great
thoughts and do great things.

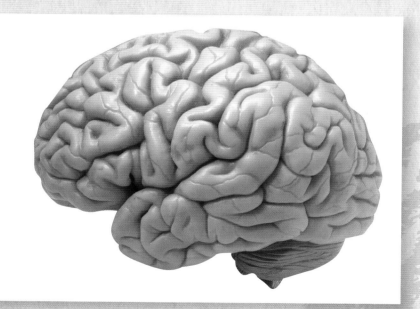

Uncle Joshua looks disappointed, and there's a kind of sadness in his eyes. "Skin's got nothing to do with what's in your head. Or your heart. Nothing at all."

But recently, Njabulo has started to think that people's skin colour does matter ... a lot.

7

"Why do people come in so many different colours anyway?"

Njabulo wonders to himself.

It's all around him – this feeling that people are different from each other. At school, he sees kids who speak different languages, live in different areas, eat different food and have different skin colours.

And if they're all so different, how are they supposed to understand each other and get along?

That's kind of why he's worried about today's meeting. Everyone in his group looks ... different.

Why so many colours?

Melanin is a natural sunscreen that protects us from harmful ultraviolet radiation (UVR) produced by the sun. Some people have a lot of it and some people have a little.

Our ancestors all lived under strong sunlight near the equator in Africa. They gained melanin in their skin through evolution in order to prevent important vitamins in their blood from being broken down by UVR.

When people started to live farther away from the equator, they lost some of their melanin sunscreen and became lighter in colour in the weaker sunlight. A little UVR is good for us because it makes vitamin D in our skin, and we need it to keep our bones and immune systems strong.

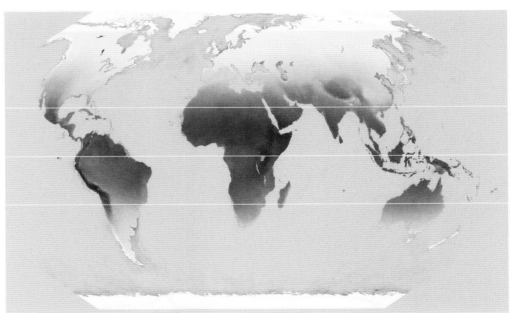

Some famous black people

Many South Africans have made a mark on world history through their intellect, courage, and innovative approaches to human problems.

Nelson Mandela

Thuli Madonsela

Siya Xuza

Desmond Tutu

Albertina Sisulu

Trevor Noah

It's hard not to believe certain things about certain people, just because of the colour of their skin. But maybe Uncle Joshua does have a point. Njabulo has never really thought about it, but how would skin affect what's on the inside? The colour of someone's skin can't affect the size of their brain, surely?

Njabulo thinks about some of the people he's learnt about that he admires – people who look like him. They are all super-clever, that's for sure!

"Hey, Njabulo!" a voice shouts from across the street.

It's Chris, and he's the first to arrive. Njabulo is glad – Chris has a bright smile and a wicked sense of humour.

"Hey," Njabulo replies shyly. "Welcome to Uncle Joshua's scrapyard."

"Wow!" says Chris excitedly as Njabulo shows him around the yard. "This is perfect – we'll find everything we need here. Thanks for having us, Njabulo!"

Just then, Aisha and Roshni come in through the gate. Aisha's mom waves as she drives off.

"Thanks for SMSing the directions, Njabulo," Roshni says. "We found it perfectly."

"And here are the project notes from Mr Leon," says Aisha, handing around some papers. "I printed them out at home. Mr Leon wants our group to make something useful out of recycled materials, and then apply what we make in a way that is socially relevant."

"Wow – trust Mr Leon to make sure we don't relax too much this weekend!" says Chris, quickly scanning the page. "So, um … any ideas?"

"How about making musical instruments?" Njabulo says. In the many hours he has spent here in Uncle Joshua's scrapyard, he's discovered all kinds of uses for the things lying around. This could be fun, after all!

Just then Tim arrives, and the others fill him in on the plan.

"Cool!" Tim says, grabbing a tin-can drum and thumping the lid with the palms of his hands. "I like it – let's make some noise!" Roshni picks up some sticks and experiments with hitting them on car parts that are hanging on a wire. Each part makes its own special ringing sound, and soon she has a melody going.

On another drum, Aisha starts to create a beat. Soft and rushing, it sounds like waves lapping against rocks in the quiet of an early morning. Chris joins in with a clanging bass sound as he knocks two metal pipes together.

Before he knows it, Njabulo finds himself tapping out the rhythm against his leg. Grinning at each other, the children carry on for a few more minutes, feeling out the sound before the music comes to a natural stop.

"Hey, guys – that sounds great! Anyone thirsty?" Uncle Joshua has appeared with some cans of cooldrink, and everyone nods gratefully.

Njabulo proudly introduces his uncle, "Everyone, this is Uncle Joshua. Uncle Joshua, this is … everyone."

"Well, it looks as though we've figured out the recycling part of the project!" Aisha says brightly as they help themselves to the drinks.

"But now we need a theme – something 'socially relevant,'" adds Roshni, rolling her eyes.

For a moment, no one says a word. Then:

"I might have an idea for you," Uncle Joshua says thoughtfully. "It's something I was just wondering ... Why do humans come in so many different colours?"

"Oh, that's easy!" says Tim. "We inherit our genes from our parents."

Uncle Joshua nods. "Sure, but where did it start? How did your parents' parents' parents get the colour they passed on?"

No one answers.

"Did you know it all began right here in Africa?" Uncle Joshua says. "A very long time ago, all people lived in Africa ..."

Skin colour genes

Everyone has genes that determine the colour of their skin. Because skin colour is important for survival, the activity of skin colour genes has been directed through natural selection.

Dark skin with lots of melanin is important for people living under strong sunlight, and the genes controlling melanin production have been under strict genetic control. Light skin with little melanin is important for people living under weak sunlight, and their skin colour genes reflect the importance of depigmentation in order to promote making vitamin D.

People who live under seasonal sunlight have the ability to tan, and this is directed by different sets of colour genes.

So many genes!

There are more than 100 genes that control human skin colour! Some of these genes are more important and some are less important. Generally, these genes do not influence the appearance of other traits. Rather, eye colour, hair colour, hair texture, and other features are controlled by different sets of genes.

We inherit our skin colour genes from our parents, but it's hard to predict what colour any child will be because genes from their parents combine in complex ways during reproduction.

That's why brothers and sisters sometimes have different colour skin even though they have the same parents. Girls tend to be a little lighter than boys. This is probably because, when they grow up, they will need to make enough vitamin D for their babies if they are pregnant.

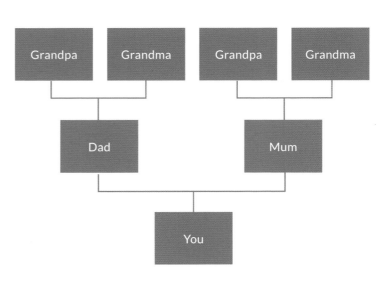

Chris scratches his head, Roshni frowns and the others look surprised as Uncle Joshua continues.

"Africa has always had a hot climate, and human skin is very clever – it makes its own sunscreen to protect us from the sun's rays. The darker a person's skin, the more melanin they have. The first people, the people who lived here in Africa, they were all dark-skinned."

"But, Uncle Joshua," Aisha interrupts, "both Njabulo and I are African. How come we have different coloured skins?"

"Well, a lot has changed in the time since then – and that's an interesting story! It's a story of how human genes adapted to different places over a very long time. And it's the genes we get from our parents that give us our individual skin colour."

19

"Is that also why we have different types of hair?" Roshni asks, looking at the others.

"Sharp!" Uncle Joshua chuckles. "It's all about the genes you inherit. Believe it or not, even further back in time, people were once as hairy as chimpanzees! But when the conditions in our environment changed, we lost most of our hair, except for the hair on our heads. And we got protective dark skin instead. The human body is amazing like that!"

Losing our hair

We lost most of the hair on our bodies a very long time ago, probably around 2 million years ago when our long-legged ancestors started to stride and run over open ground in search of food.

We lost our body hair and developed more sweat glands at the same time, and this helped us to keep our bodies at an even temperature, even when we were working hard in the sun.

We kept hair on our heads, probably because it helped to protect our scalp from the direct sun and helped to keep our big brains cool. As people moved around the world, the texture and colour of their hair changed too.

"But where did these genes come from?" Njabulo asks quietly. "Why do we have all these different shades of skin now?"

"Well, that's part of the amazing human story," says Uncle Joshua, his deep voice rumbling. "Over a long period of time, the people who moved to hotter places in Africa developed darker skin. People who went to cooler places in the continent lost some of their pigment, and their skin became lighter."

Looking at the beautiful children in front of him, Uncle Joshua smiles.

Meetings of minds and colours

All the people in the world originally came from Africa, even the earliest ancestors of people who now live in Europe and Asia.

For thousands of years during the last Ice Age, most people lived in small groups, and many groups were isolated from one another. When the climate started to get warmer, people in many places started farming. Groups got bigger and people who had once been isolated came into contact with one another.

One of the main places where this happened was along the Nile River in Northern Africa, beginning around 8 000 years ago.

Dark-skinned people from southern Egypt and Sudan met and traded with lighter-skinned people from the Nile delta. They met as equals. Their skin colour didn't matter. Wars were fought, but they weren't based on colour.

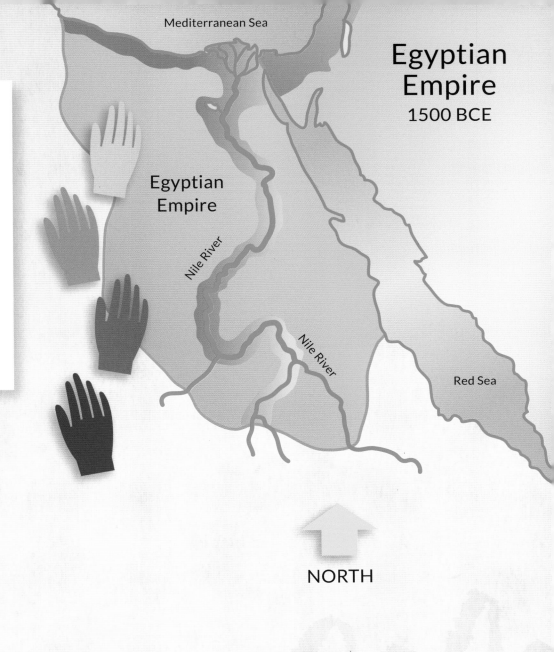

Mediterranean Sea

Egyptian Empire
1500 BCE

Egyptian Empire

Nile River

Nile River

Red Sea

NORTH

23

MOST INTENSE

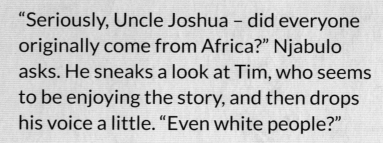

"Seriously, Uncle Joshua – did everyone originally come from Africa?" Njabulo asks. He sneaks a look at Tim, who seems to be enjoying the story, and then drops his voice a little. "Even white people?"

"Of course!" says Uncle Joshua. "That's part of the story too. People spread out across the world from their first home in Africa, changing and adapting to the environment as they moved towards Europe, Asia, the Americas and Australasia. In each place they found very different conditions, and they passed on their adapting genes to their children through many, many, many generations."

UVR INTENSITY

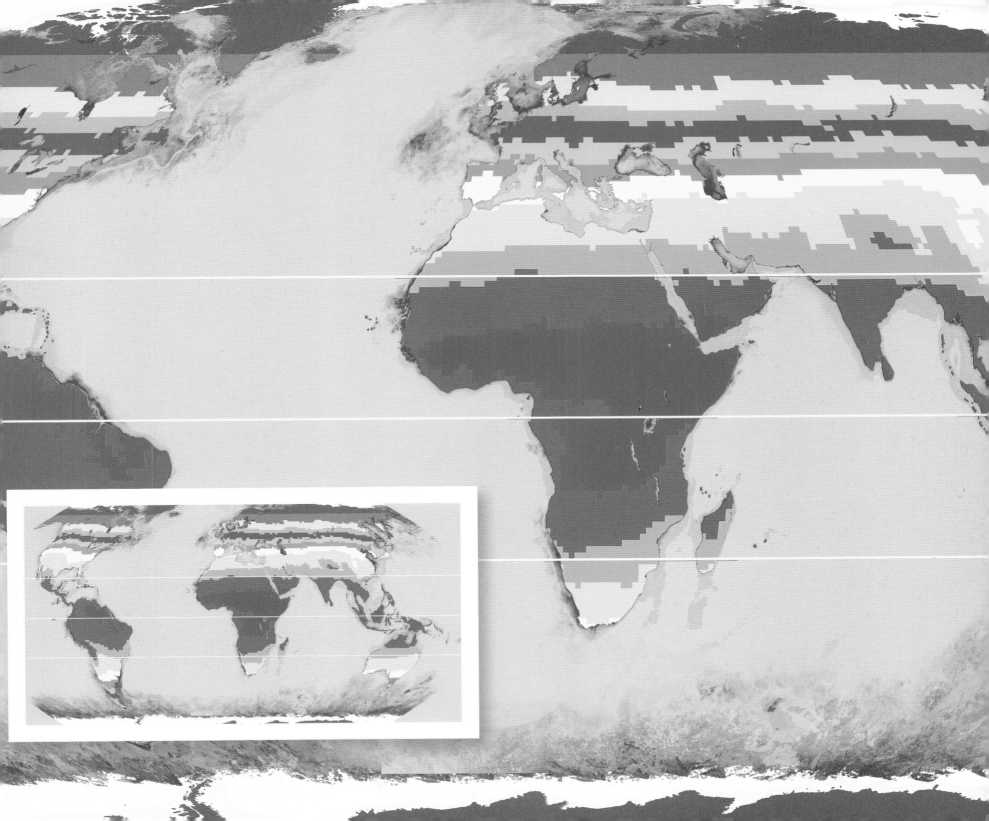

"Away from the hot African sun, in places where there was less sunlight, people did not need as much natural sunscreen. And guess what! Their skin made less sunscreen, and became lighter."

"Hmm," Chris says thoughtfully. "Tim's got light skin, but he lives here in Africa, not in Iceland!"

Everyone bursts out laughing and Tim's cheeks go bright pink.

Uncle Joshua laughs too. "Tim is recent history, my man! We're talking thousands and thousands and thousands of years ago. We're talking back when there were no airplanes, no cars, no phones ..."

"No TV?" adds Chris, helpfully.

"No TV."

Moving to higher latitudes

When some ancient Africans started to move far away from the equator, they encountered weaker and more seasonal sunshine. Over generations, their skin became lighter. Genetic changes or mutations in pigmentation genes produced less melanin so that vitamin D could be made more easily in places with less sunlight. People back then lived outside and didn't move very far during their lifetimes, and so their skin colour was well suited to the environments in which they lived.

Things changed a lot in the last 4,000 years though, because many of us now live far from our ancestral homelands and if we live in towns and cities, we spend a lot of time indoors. This means that today some of us have skin that no longer matches our environments. This can lead to health problems, especially when our bodies don't get enough vitamin D.

"Not even Khumbul'ekhaya?" Njabulo asks with a twinkle in his eye.

"Hey, that TV show might reconnect long-lost relatives every Wednesday night," says Uncle Joshua, "but back then, there was no contact between the groups of people who had migrated to different places in the world.

Remember, people had to walk wherever they wanted to go, so it took many, many, many generations for people to spread all over the world. They were driven by all kind of factors, like food, water, shelter. Meantime, languages changed, cultures changed, traditions changed and skin changed – all in response to the different environments people found themselves in."

What was it like back then?

We think that our grandparents are old, but our species of modern people – Homo sapiens – has been around for 200,000 years! People only started wearing sewn clothing about 20,000 years ago. They started using wheels and metal tools only around 5,000 years ago.

For most of history people stayed at home, and their waking hours were spent out of doors. Because they didn't live in buildings, they experienced the change of seasons with their bodies. They spoke beautiful languages but weren't able to write.

Living in small, widely separated groups, people sometimes had to walk long distances to find food or meet relatives. The climate in many places was cold and dry. Life was hard.

"So that's why we all have different coloured skin – because in all these different places people found themselves in, they needed different kinds of protection from the sun?" Njabulo says.

Uncle Joshua nods. "Remember our little friend on the tree branch?"

"The chameleon?"

"Same principle. Why don't you tell your friends what you saw?"

Njabulo explains to the others how the chameleon had changed from brown to green as it had moved from a dry stalk to a leaf.

Our adventurous and inventive ancestors

Around 50,000 years ago, people everywhere started to be even more creative and resourceful. People's tools became more sophisticated, and they began to make art and jewellery. New languages and cultures developed, and people moved far and wide across the world.

It was an amazing time when people faced enormous challenges in unknown landscapes, with new animals and plants around them. But our ancestors were excellent observers of nature and were able to solve problems through their intelligence and creativity. Our big brains made it possible for us to survive and thrive!

31

"The chameleon uses its skin colour to protect itself," Uncle Joshua says. "Its clever skin takes on the colour of its environment to help it to hide."

The children nod, impressed by how the chameleon is able to keep itself safe.

"The problem is," Uncle Joshua continues, "while people's genes were changing in response to their changing environments, they lost contact with each other. People also didn't know how to read or write yet, and there was no other form of communication between groups – no books or newspapers. So no one had any idea what other people in the world were up to, or what they looked like. When technology improved, and people started being able to travel large distances, they were pretty surprised to meet up with people who looked so different from them!"

More new skin colours

In the last few thousand years, people have developed ways to move easily and quickly from one part of the world to another. More and more people have relocated, sometimes out of choice, sometimes against their will. And wherever they go, people get married and have babies.

As modern people move around from one continent or country to another and mix together, the world is filling with new skin colours and new combinations of pigmentation genes. In big cities, we can often see every imaginable shade of brown. This human rainbow is a result of our progress and is something to be celebrated.

33

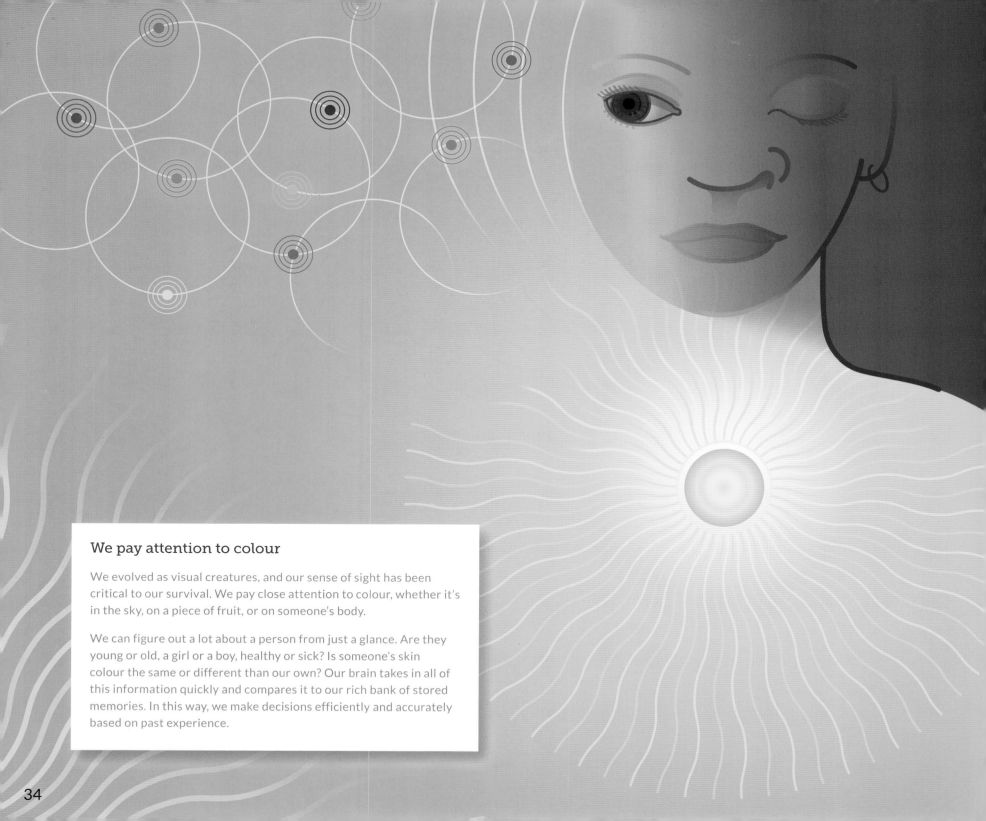

We pay attention to colour

We evolved as visual creatures, and our sense of sight has been critical to our survival. We pay close attention to colour, whether it's in the sky, on a piece of fruit, or on someone's body.

We can figure out a lot about a person from just a glance. Are they young or old, a girl or a boy, healthy or sick? Is someone's skin colour the same or different than our own? Our brain takes in all of this information quickly and compares it to our rich bank of stored memories. In this way, we make decisions efficiently and accurately based on past experience.

Uncle Joshua takes a sip from his bottle of water.

"Skin colour is a very visible difference. It's easy to see someone's skin colour – it might even be the first thing you notice about a person. What you can't see is the person inside that skin. Apart from telling you what colour genes the person has inherited from his or her ancestors, skin colour tells you nothing about who the person is inside."

He lets that sink in.

"You have to get to know someone to understand how they think or behave, what they care about and who they love. You have to know someone to understand who they are."

There's a sad smile on Uncle Joshua's face.

"Problem is, around the eighteenth century, some European men of great learning decided it was a good idea to rank people according to the colour of their skin. Back then people didn't know what we know now – that the skin's just an organ adapted to a particular environment. To the visible difference of skin, they added the invisible difference of value. And they put white people like themselves at the top of the pile."

36

"Had they forgotten that they also came from Africa?" Njabulo asks.

Uncle Joshua sighs. "Somewhere along the way, people forgot that we are all cousins from an ancient African ancestor. And so often we react to difference simply because we are fearful of what we don't know or understand. "

Immanuel Kant
(1724-1804)

David Hume
(1711-1776)

Who says your skin colour is better than mine?

People have always noticed skin colour. What has changed is how people think about skin colour. Long ago, Europeans associated light skin colours with virtue, intelligence and goodness, and dark colours with immorality, stupidity and evil.

But maybe they were just scared of people who looked different to them. Most of these men had no experience with people from different places, who spoke different languages from them.Some of them travelled the world to look for economic opportunities, and came into contact with people who looked different from them. Sometimes they wanted the dark-skinned people in these places to work for them for as little pay as possible. It suited them to think of these people in a certain way and deprive them of basic human rights.

All over the world, we are still living with the consequences of European colonisation.

He looks pointedly at Njabulo. The sun is dipping in the late-afternoon light, and soon the children will be going home.

"So, my boy, now can you think of a theme for your recycling project?" Then he leans over so that only Njabulo can hear him, and whispers, "And do you still want to change your skin like a chameleon?"

Njabulo grins. "No, Uncle Joshua. As you say, skin colour doesn't make us who we are. And it's cool to think we all originally come from the same place, no matter what we look like!"

There is silence in the scrap yard as everyone thinks about this for a moment. Then ...

Skin we are in!

Our skin is important, but it's also just the covering for our bodies. Our different skin colours have helped people survive in different places under different conditions, but it isn't related to what's in their minds and hearts.

In fact, whoever started calling people "black" and "white" can't see that we are all beautiful shades of brown.

People are clever, strong and resilient. We can climb mountains, make music, solve equations and dance! We may speak many languages, but we all seek happiness and security for ourselves and our children. Let's enjoy the skin we are in, knowing that our real selves are within our skin!

39

"Hey, that sounds like a song to me," says Roshni. She grabs a stick and starts tapping on her strung-up car parts.

Rippity-tap, rippity- tap ...

Tim and Aisha begin drumming, their two tin-cans creating a rich double beat. Then they begin to hum along. Chris soon joins in, banging together two pipes, and then Njabulo does what he does best: rapping to the beat, telling the story of skin.

And in no time at all, the group is in full swing.

Understanding skin colour matters

When we understand why we have our skin colour, we can appreciate the good job evolution did to equip us to live in all kinds of places. We'll be healthier too because we'll make sure that we play outside and eat the right things to keep our bodies strong.

All people will be happier and the world will be a better place when we all understand that colour doesn't change who we really are. We can study, play and be good to one another. Knowing the story of the skin we are in, we'll truly be free!

The Skin Song

Look at our skin,
See all the colours –
Black, brown, white,
And all the others

But though my skin's
A source of pride,
It doesn't show
What's on the inside!

My clever skin
Knows how to adapt,
But it's just the package
In which I'm wrapped

And although it's the first thing
That you see
It's not the most important
Part of me.

We all have feelings,
Thoughts and fears,
We all learn and grow
Through the years.

We may look different
With different hues
But here's a cool
Bit of news:

My skin comes from my genes
Through the ages
Via my ancestors
From different places

Skin protects us from the sun –
That's where it starts –
But it doesn't make a
difference
To what's in our hearts.

Luister goed! Mamela, wena!
Listen carefully, dear friend –
Skin's the beginning,
It's not the end.

Maak'ie saak'ie
Makes no difference
Ayithethi nto tu